DARWIN'S
VOYAGE OF DISCOVERY

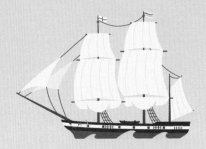

To all my friends and family for their continued love and support – Jake Williams

Many thanks to Mandy Archer for helping with the text on this book

First published in the United Kingdom in 2019 by
Pavilion Children's Books
43 Great Ormond Street
London
WC1N 3HZ

An imprint of Pavilion Books Company Limited

Publisher and editor: Neil Dunnicliffe
Assistant editor: Harriet Grylls
Art director and designer: Lee-May Lim

ISBN: 9781843654148

A CIP catalogue record for this book is available from the British Library.

10 9 8 7 6 5 4 3 2 1

Reproduction by Rival Colour Ltd., UK
Printed by 1010 Printing International Ltd, China.

This book can be ordered directly from the publisher online
at www.pavilionbooks.com, or try your local bookshop.

DARWIN'S VOYAGE OF DISCOVERY

JAKE WILLIAMS

PAVILION

A natural wonder

Charles Robert Darwin was born on 12 February 1809. His family were wealthy and respectable people from Shrewsbury, England. Charles' mother, Susannah, died when he was only eight years old. After that, his three elder sisters helped to raise and care for him. Charles' father, Robert, was loving but very strict.

Charles' grandfather was Erasmus Darwin, a famous philosopher, and his father was a doctor. During his early years however, Charles' own brilliance didn't immediately shine through. Few could have realised that he would grow up to become one of the greatest scientists that ever lived.

Although Charles wasn't particularly good at schoolwork, he always loved nature. He liked to spend hours roaming around outside, examining plants and insects, and seeking out shells, birds' eggs and pebbles. One of the earliest drawings of Charles shows him clutching a plant that he had been growing in a pot.

When Charles turned nine, he was sent off to boarding school. By now his passion for natural history was clear. At times he became frustrated at having to study subjects like Latin and Greek classics when he would much rather have been learning about botany and geology.

During his youth, Charles enjoyed many hobbies. He liked to go bird-watching, read books and build all sorts of collections. He and his big brother even set up a homemade chemistry laboratory in a garden shed! Charles later described their experiments in the lab as the best part of his school education.

Growing up

Charles dreamed of a career in biology or natural history, but his father had other ideas. When he was just sixteen, he was enrolled at Edinburgh University to study medicine. Poor Charles greatly disliked his new subject.

If he was going to be a doctor, Charles would need to perform operations. At the time, patients weren't put to sleep or given pain relief to help them cope with medical procedures. Charles was shocked by the blood, gore and suffering that occurred during surgery – he gave up his studies without finishing the course.

After Charles left Edinburgh, his father proposed a career working for the Church of England instead. Charles was dispatched to Christ's College, Cambridge, to train to become a clergyman. While he was there, Charles met a botany professor called John Stevens Henslow. The pair soon became very close friends.

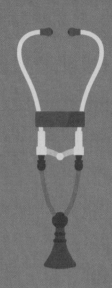

A colourful collection

Charles wasn't especially religious and was in no hurry to go into the Church. Life at Cambridge did have one advantage, however – after classes there was plenty of time to discuss science with Professor Henslow, go walking in the countryside and add to his beetle collection. Charles searched far and wide for rare and interesting species. His collection would become so extensive that scientists are still finding new species within it today, nearly 200 years later.

The Invitation

In August 1831, Professor Henslow sent Charles a very special letter. Its contents would start a chain of events that would not only change his life, but influence the sciences, and wider society, for centuries to come. The letter was an invitation to join the crew of a ship about to embark on a surveying voyage around the world. The captain was searching for a naturalist to come on the journey. Henslow had put Charles' name forward. Rather than search for a job within the Church, Charles immediately set out to persuade his father to let him go to sea. Dr Darwin was dismayed – he thought it was a foolish idea.

A long voyage

The ship was called HMS *Beagle*. Captain Robert FitzRoy was in command, a young naval officer who was keen to find a gentleman companion with an interest in science. The plotted course would cover nearly 65,000 kilometres, all the way around the circumference of the globe. Whilst the *Beagle* crew surveyed the coastline and made maps, Darwin would be able to travel inland to study exotic plants and wildlife from around the world.

Charles needed help – he didn't just have to persuade his father to let him go on the voyage, he would have to put up the money to pay for it, too. Luckily his uncle Josiah stepped in. He wrote to Charles' father, urging him to reconsider. At last, Dr Darwin agreed.

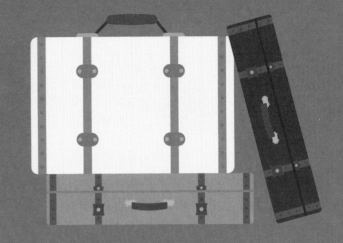

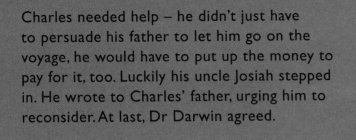

Now Charles could not wait to set sail on the journey of a lifetime! As the departure date drew closer, he went down to Cambridge to visit Professor Henslow. Charles also headed to London to meet with Captain FitzRoy.

HMS *Beagle*

Britain's navy was considered the strongest and most respected in the world. In order to maintain this status, it required the very best maps and sea charts. HMS *Beagle* was one of several small ships used to make detailed surveys of coasts and oceans across the globe. It had made its first voyage between 1826 and 1830.

⟵ 27 metres ⟶

HMS *Beagle* was around 27 metres long – about the same as two buses parked end to end.

The *Beagle* was commissioned to map the coast of South America. The ship had become very damaged during its first expedition and needed major repair work. While this was going on, Charles consulted with scientists in London and bought supplies. Everything had to be carefully prepared – the hull was treated so it was watertight, ropes were replaced and the decks were scrubbed.

HMS *Beagle* was not a warship, but it had to be ready to deal with danger. Who knew what it might encounter when sailing far from home in unchartered waters? A number of the crew were navy marines – armed sailors trained to defend the ship from pirates, enemy ships or worse.

The ship originally had 10 cannons. For Darwin's expedition it had six.

Compact and cosy

Life below deck on the *Beagle* was cramped, but the crew certainly made the most of the limited space. The ship had all the essentials a traveller could need for an around-the-world journey, from food halls to mess rooms and coal storage.

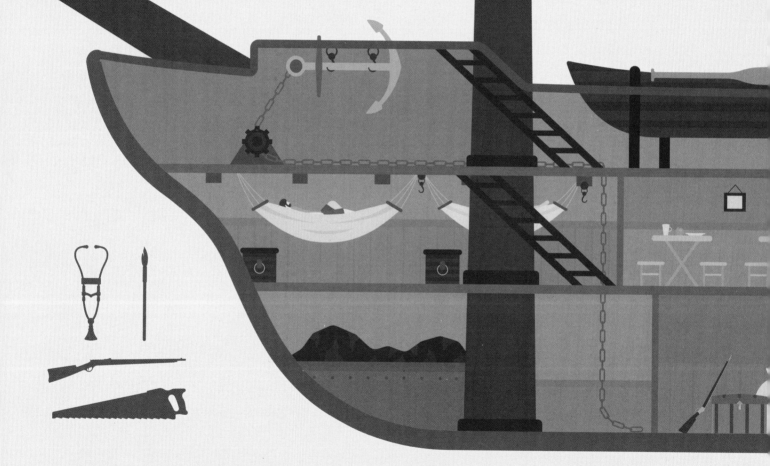

Home improvements

As part of his repair work, Captain FitzRoy raised the rear deck of the ship by around 1.5m, creating a new level called the 'poop deck'. The increased height of the poop deck made it easier for the crew to navigate and view the area around them. The chart room was located underneath the poop deck. This is where the crew would come together to examine maps and help plot the course of the ship. It was also the space where Charles would sleep during the voyage, hooking a hammock up above the chart table each evening.

Living on such a small ship for weeks or even months at a time, Charles probably explored every inch of the vessel during his time aboard. Although he slept in the tiny chart room, as a gentleman he would be expected to take his meals with the Captain.

Kit list

As soon as his father agreed to pay for the *Beagle* expedition, Charles began packing and shopping for the trip. There would be limited space on-board, so he had to consider very carefully what equipment he could bring. There were some hard choices to make – the voyage was planned to last for at least two years.

Club

For protection against hostile strangers.

Knife

Useful for making plant cuttings out in the field.

Bible

Charles still intended to become a clergyman when he got home.

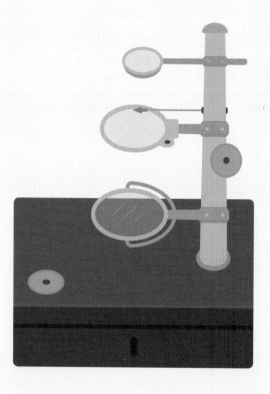

Microscope

Essential for studying specimens in close-up.

Telescope

Necessary to see objects far away, and one of Charles' most expensive and precious pieces of equipment.

Acid test kit

Charles' scientific instruments allowed him to test and analyse samples on-board ship.

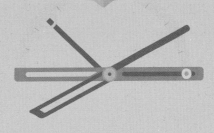

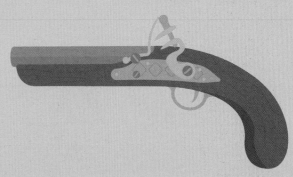

Geological hammer

For chipping off small slivers of rock and stone.

Goniometer

A device used to accurately gauge the shape of crystals in minerals.

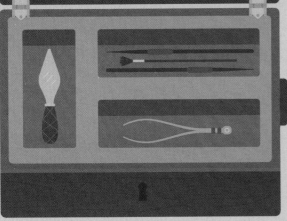
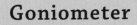

Pistol

Another important item to help Charles stay safe.

Clinometer

A special compass that can measure the angle of mountain slopes.

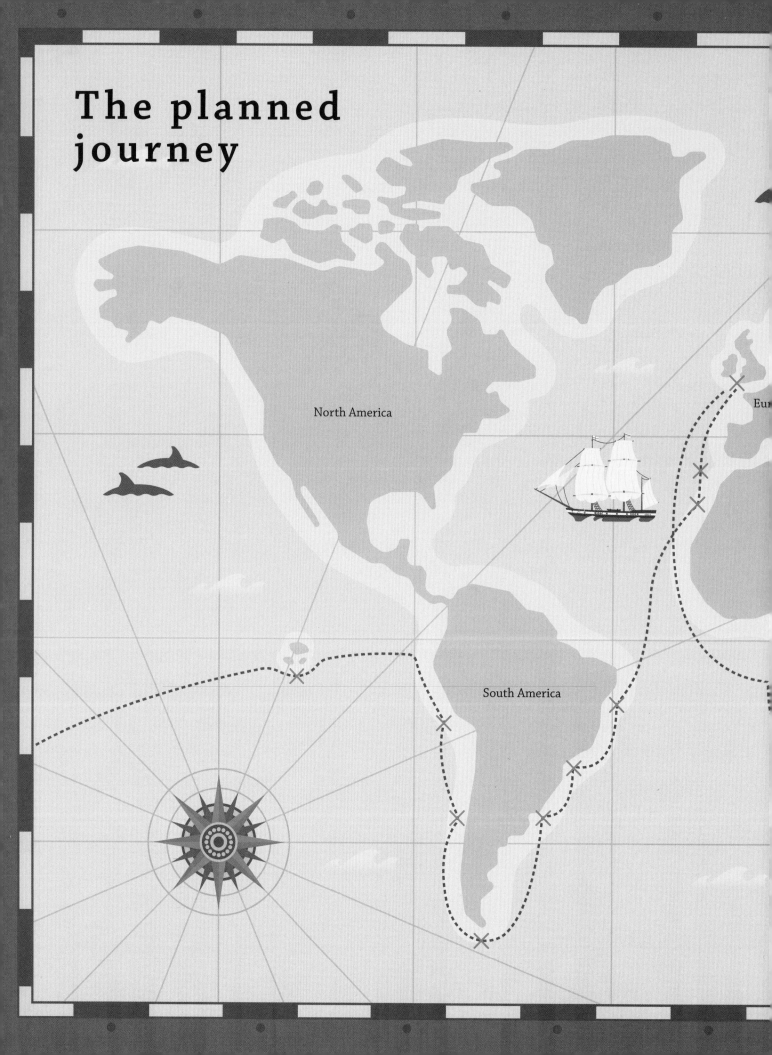

The planned journey

North America

South America

Eur

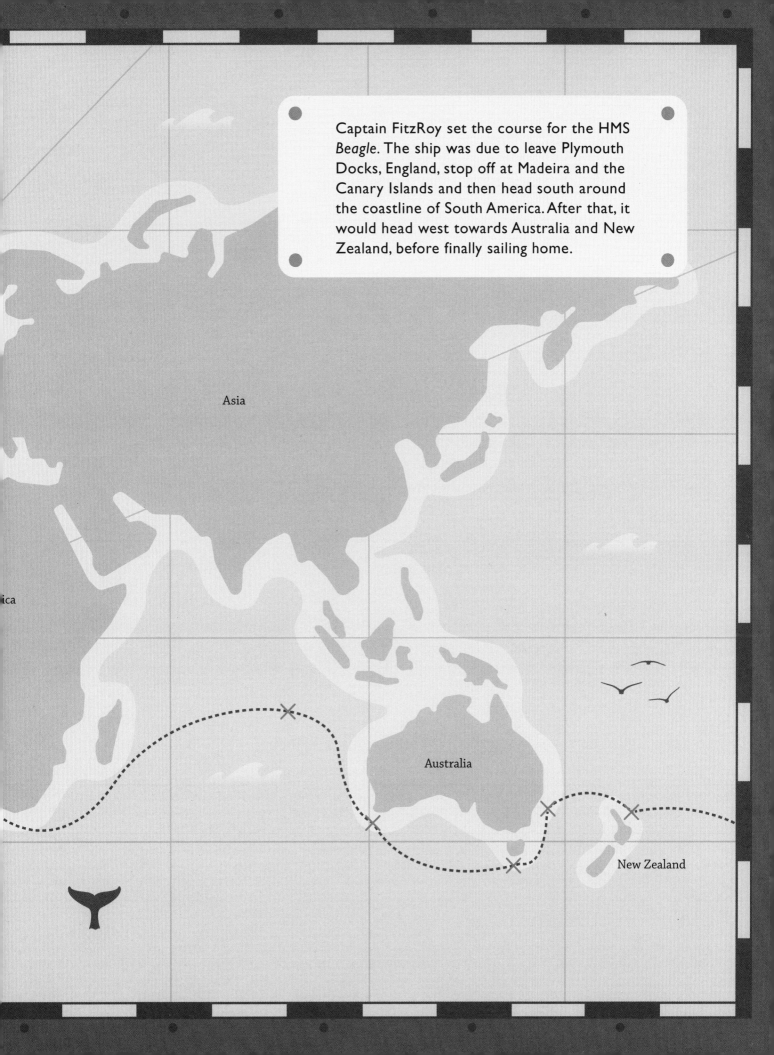

Captain FitzRoy set the course for the HMS *Beagle*. The ship was due to leave Plymouth Docks, England, stop off at Madeira and the Canary Islands and then head south around the coastline of South America. After that, it would head west towards Australia and New Zealand, before finally sailing home.

Asia

ica

Australia

New Zealand

Dawn of an adventure

Captain FitzRoy was a skilled and able seaman, but the *Beagle's* second voyage didn't get off to a brilliant start. Charles and the crew were ready to board ship in October 1831, only to be grounded in Plymouth for weeks due to bad weather. The ship tried to set off twice, but gale force winds obliged FitzRoy to turn back into harbour.

Off at last

As Christmas approached, the weather finally improved. On a calm, drizzly morning on 27 December 1831, FitzRoy gave the order to set sail. Charles Darwin's epic adventure had begun! Although the voyage was planned to last two years, he and the 73 others on-board would not see England again for nearly five.

Second thoughts

As the days turned into weeks and then months, Charles began to wonder if the expedition was really such a good idea. He started to get pains in his chest and heart flutters. He wrote in his diary that it was the most miserable time he had ever spent.

The voyage begins

Sea legs

From the moment the *Beagle* left England, Charles became terribly seasick. The crew worked hard, raising the sails and adjusting the ship's course to make the most of the weather conditions. If anyone disobeyed the captain, they were harshly punished.

Home from home?

Charles struggled to cope with spending night after night out on the ocean. Sometimes he felt so poorly, all he could do was shut himself in his cabin. He stayed there for hours on end, lying in his hammock. The Atlantic Ocean had many strong currents and fierce winds.

Stormy seas

FitzRoy steered the ship down towards the west coast of Africa. The first stop was planned for the island of Madeira, but stormy weather prevented the *Beagle* from docking. There was no choice but to sail on to the next friendly port!

Raisins and biscuits

Charles' seasickness lasted for the entire voyage. During the early stages of the journey, the only foods he could keep down were raisins and biscuits. He must have felt very glum. At times when he did feel better, Charles used the hours at sea to read books and think.

Can't stop here

After Madeira, Captain FitzRoy plotted a course for the Canary Islands. Charles had arranged to meet a friend there and go exploring together, but again it was not to be. News arrived of a cholera outbreak back in England. The men were not allowed ashore in case they were carrying the disease. Charles must have wondered where this voyage would take him next...

Astounding animals

Charles could never have imagined the wonders that were waiting for him on his *Beagle* adventure. A dazzling array of breathtaking creatures – from huge, lumbering tortoises to bizarre web-footed platypuses and the tiniest, glossy insects – would all play their part in shaping the most astounding scientific theory the world had ever known. It would eventually be known as Darwin's theory of evolution.

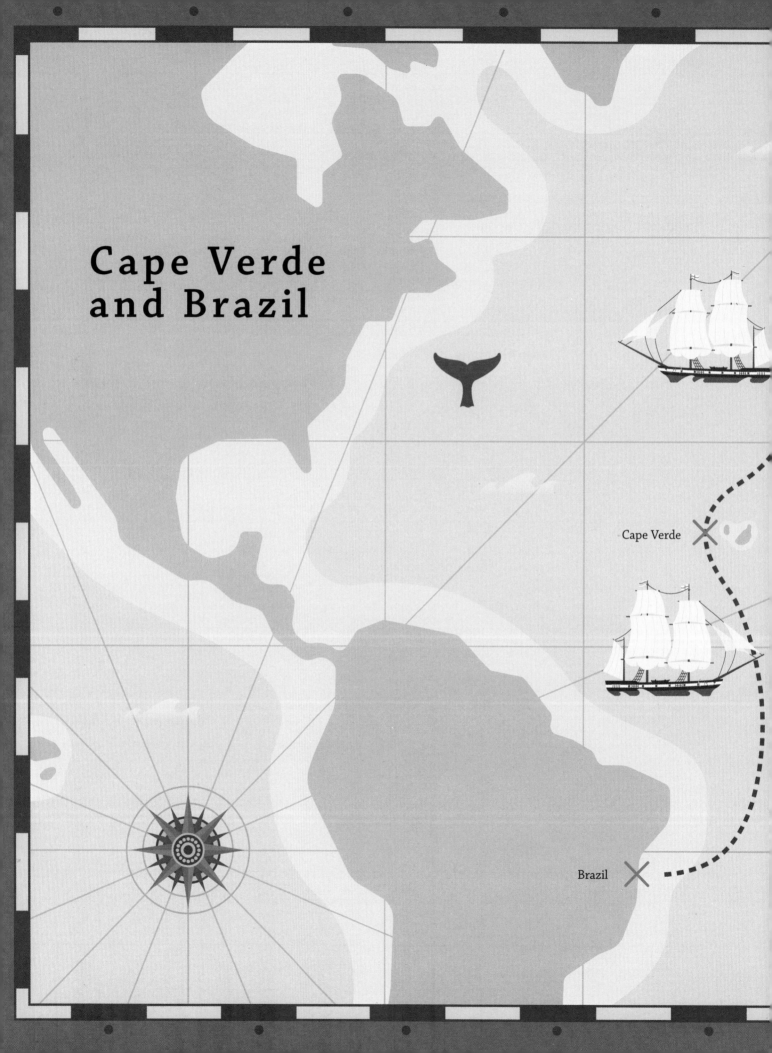

Cape Verde and Brazil

Cape Verde

Brazil

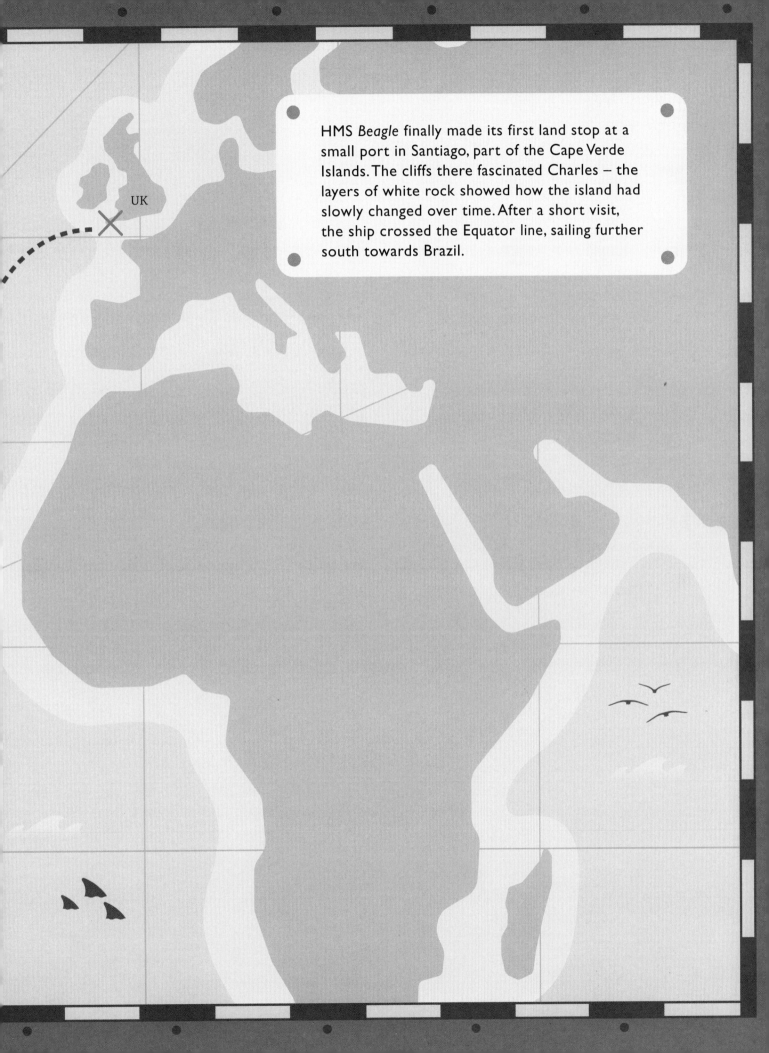

UK

HMS *Beagle* finally made its first land stop at a small port in Santiago, part of the Cape Verde Islands. The cliffs there fascinated Charles – the layers of white rock showed how the island had slowly changed over time. After a short visit, the ship crossed the Equator line, sailing further south towards Brazil.

Curious cuttlefish

As soon as Charles started exploring Santiago, his misery turned to delight. This new tropical landscape was filled with lush plants, beautiful beaches and astonishing wildlife! One day, when he was out swimming he came face to face with a common cuttlefish – a rubbery sea creature with a tentacled face and a rippling fin.

Take that!

Sometimes while he was observing the cuttlefish, Charles got splashed with water. The creature has the ability to suck liquid into its body – and then squirt it out again, fast! When a cuttlefish senses danger, it uses the jet to propel its body through the sea and make a quick getaway.

Colour me clever

Cuttlefish are related to squid and octopuses. Charles was amazed at the incredible skills the species had developed to help them blend into their surroundings, escape predators and catch prey. Perhaps most jaw-dropping of all is the ability to nearly instantly change colour! Cuttlefish have transparent skin with a layer of cells underneath that expand and contract. This change in the cells causes the rapid shift in colour.

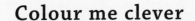

Look, but don't touch

Cuttlefish are not only able to change their body colour, they can also change texture! Their skin is able to warp from smooth to rough and spiky in less than a second. This change helps the sea creatures to blend in even better with the rocks and sand in their environment.

St Paul's Rocks

Captain FitzRoy wanted to make one more stop on the way to Brazil. HMS *Beagle* dropped anchor for just one day at St Paul's Rocks, part of a tiny crop of islands popping out of the water halfway between Africa and South America. The ridge of rocks was very dangerous for passing ships. While Charles went ashore, FitzRoy and his crew set about charting their exact shape and location.

Dawn of an idea

Charles started his research by making a list of all the wildlife that he could find on the island. There were no grass, trees or plants anywhere – just crabs, squawking sea birds and a handful of insects. The little bugs and spiders that managed to survive here got Charles thinking. Perhaps this was how life began? Did the insects come first, before larger, more complex species appeared?

A world without people

St Paul's Rocks was a remote and lonely place. It is staggering that Captain FitzRoy was even able to find it! The wind-battered ground was dotted with birds and their nests. The animals had never seen human beings before, so they weren't at all afraid. The sailors were even able to walk right up to the birds.

Noddies and boobies

There were two types of birds living on the island – the grey noddy and the brown booby. The seabirds lived in large breeding colonies. The rocks were covered with *guano* – the remains of bird dung that had hardened over centuries.

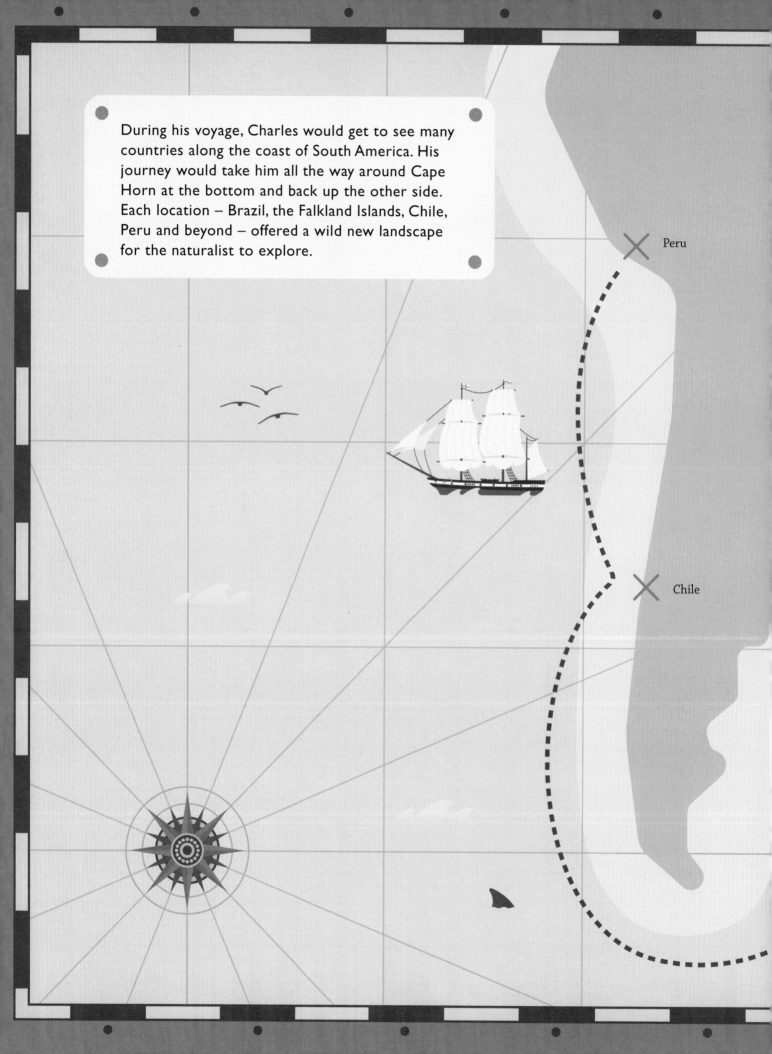

During his voyage, Charles would get to see many countries along the coast of South America. His journey would take him all the way around Cape Horn at the bottom and back up the other side. Each location – Brazil, the Falkland Islands, Chile, Peru and beyond – offered a wild new landscape for the naturalist to explore.

Peru

Chile

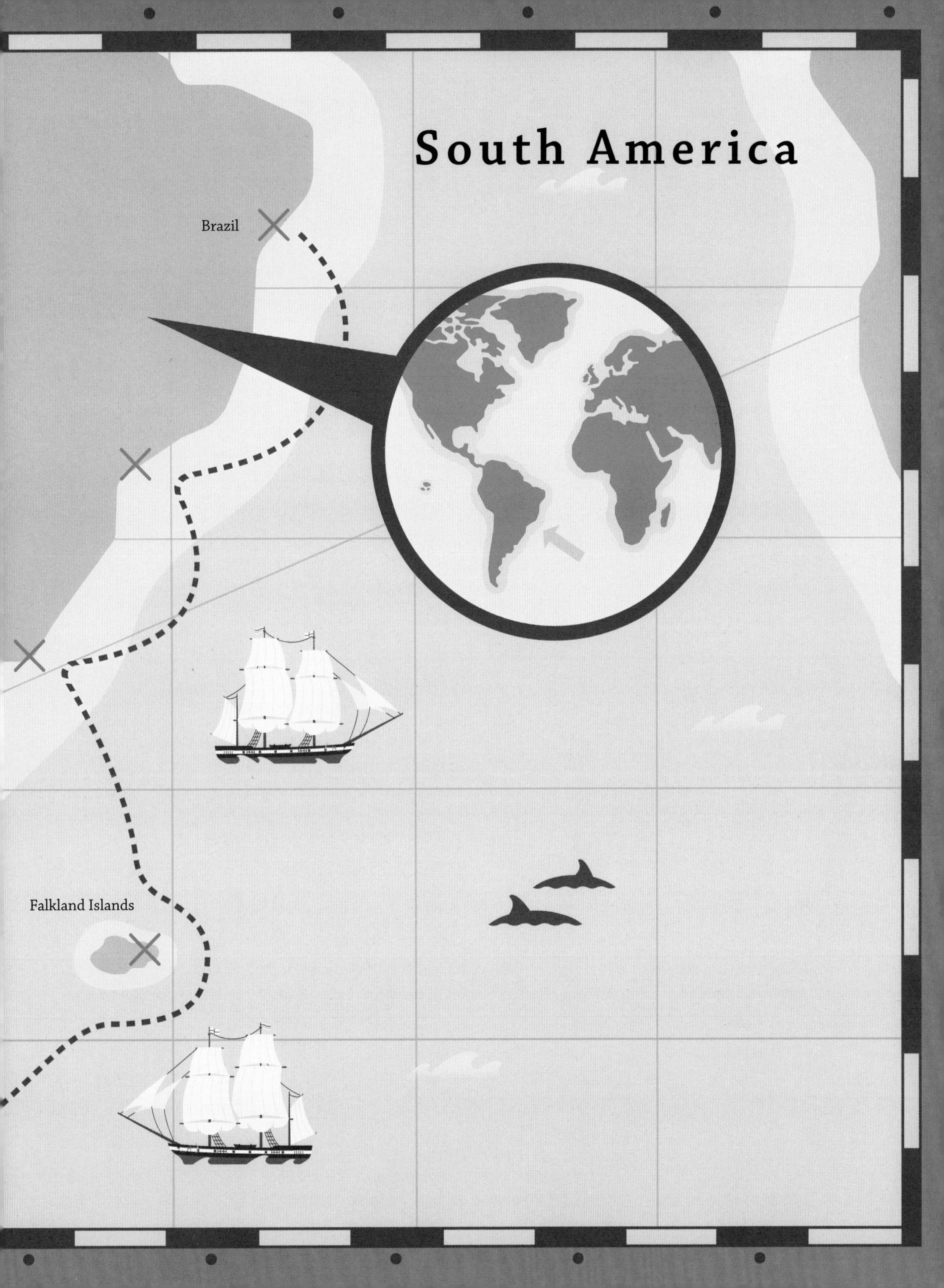

South America

Brazil

Falkland Islands

A whole new world

When Charles finally arrived in Brazil, he was in for a treat. As he hiked through the warm rainforests he described the scene as beautiful beyond his 'wildest dreams'. He immediately began making detailed notes and drawings, recording data and taking specimen samples of the plants and animals he observed, ready to send back to England.

What's that noise?

As Charles pushed aside creepers and stepped beneath the canopy of trees, he spotted many beautiful butterflies. He listened carefully as the insects made a series of clicking sounds. Charles couldn't believe his ears – it was as if the butterflies were talking to each other! Could that possibly be true?

Cracker butterflies

Charles had not been imagining things – he had chanced upon a group of butterflies that really do make noises as they fly. Even to this day, it is not entirely clear how the *Hamadryas*, or 'cracker' butterfly makes its clicking sound, although scientists are certain that they use their wings to do it.

Listen up!

Scientists now believe that the cracker butterflies use their special ability to send messages to other butterflies in the area. The clicks could be made to warn insects off their territory, to attract a mate or even to socialise with others.

Baffling birds

During his expedition around South America, Charles was interested to hear about a large, flightless bird called the rhea. The rhea looks a bit like an ostrich with a small head, a long neck and strong legs. When a rhea runs it spreads its wings out so they act as big, feathery sails.

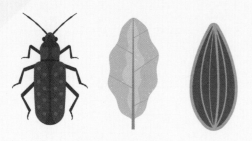

Feeling peckish

Rheas mostly eat leafy plants, fruit and seeds, but their diet also includes beetles and sometimes even larger creatures such as small lizards.

Greater and lesser rhea

The greater rhea was well known, but Charles was surprised to learn of another, smaller species. He spent some time searching for it without any luck. Then, one day, the ship's artist shot a bird to serve for dinner. As Charles looked at the bones on his plate, he realised that it had to be the rare lesser rhea!

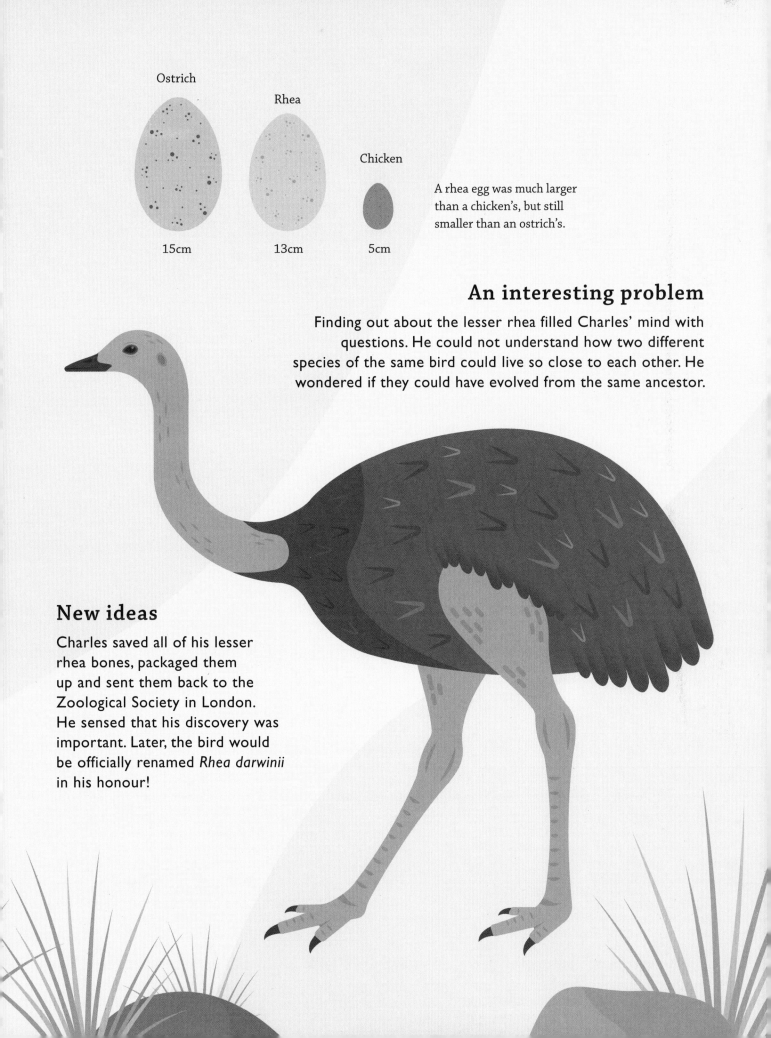

Ostrich

Rhea

Chicken

15cm

13cm

5cm

A rhea egg was much larger than a chicken's, but still smaller than an ostrich's.

An interesting problem

Finding out about the lesser rhea filled Charles' mind with questions. He could not understand how two different species of the same bird could live so close to each other. He wondered if they could have evolved from the same ancestor.

New ideas

Charles saved all of his lesser rhea bones, packaged them up and sent them back to the Zoological Society in London. He sensed that his discovery was important. Later, the bird would be officially renamed *Rhea darwinii* in his honour!

Shining brightly

Every creature that Charles observed seemed to offer a new insight into how nature worked. One of the most magical was the little firefly. In his notebook Charles remarked that they could be seen from about 200 paces distant, emitting little bursts of light.

Beetles not flies

The firefly is a small winged beetle, part of a family called Lampyridae. It's the perfect name for this sort of insect – lampyridae means 'the shining ones' in Greek. Glowworms are also in this family, but they do not have wings.

Off and on

Charles discovered that when disturbed, the fireflies were able to make a brilliant point of light that pulsed in intervals, like fairy lights switching off and on again in the darkness.

Over here!

The firefly uses its light to try and attract a mate. Each flash comes from the rings around the base of the beetle's abdomen. The light is produced by a chemical reaction inside the insect. Each different sub-species of firefly has its own unique pattern.

Luminous powers

Nowadays scientists describe the ability to emit light as bioluminescence. Glowworms, fungi, jellyfish and lots of deep-sea creatures also have this special skill. Charles was confused by what he saw. Why were some organisms able to glow in the dark when others couldn't, even if they were closely related?

Duel to the death

One day when he was exploring Rio de Janeiro, Charles came across a terrible battle. A huge, hairy tarantula was fighting to defend itself against an enormous wasp! The naturalist couldn't take his eyes off the scene, shocked to see these two different species locked in mortal combat.

Spider senses

The tarantula is a mighty spider, a fearsome predator that can easily hunt down rodents and even small birds. Yet as Charles watched the creature, it soon became clear that the tarantula was the hunted and not the hunter in this duel.

Last line of defence

When approached, the tarantula can usually scare off intruders by rising up on its back legs and exposing its sharp fangs. The wasp Charles witnessed was not to be put off so easily. It had developed a very effective way of stopping the spider in its tracks.

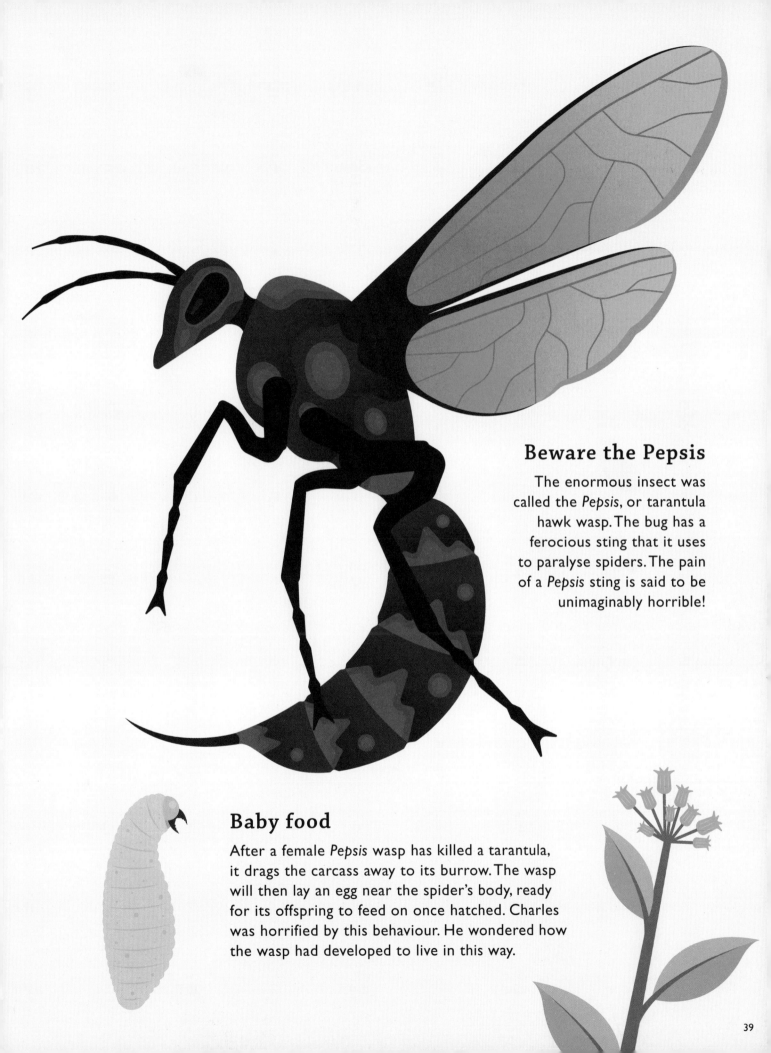

Beware the Pepsis

The enormous insect was called the *Pepsis*, or tarantula hawk wasp. The bug has a ferocious sting that it uses to paralyse spiders. The pain of a *Pepsis* sting is said to be unimaginably horrible!

Baby food

After a female *Pepsis* wasp has killed a tarantula, it drags the carcass away to its burrow. The wasp will then lay an egg near the spider's body, ready for its offspring to feed on once hatched. Charles was horrified by this behaviour. He wondered how the wasp had developed to live in this way.

Fossil finder

Charles didn't spend all of his time observing animals during his expeditions away from HMS *Beagle* – he also devoted hours to studying geology and plant life. Every corner of South America seemed to offer up a new discovery, but when Charles dug into the ground, things really started to get interesting...

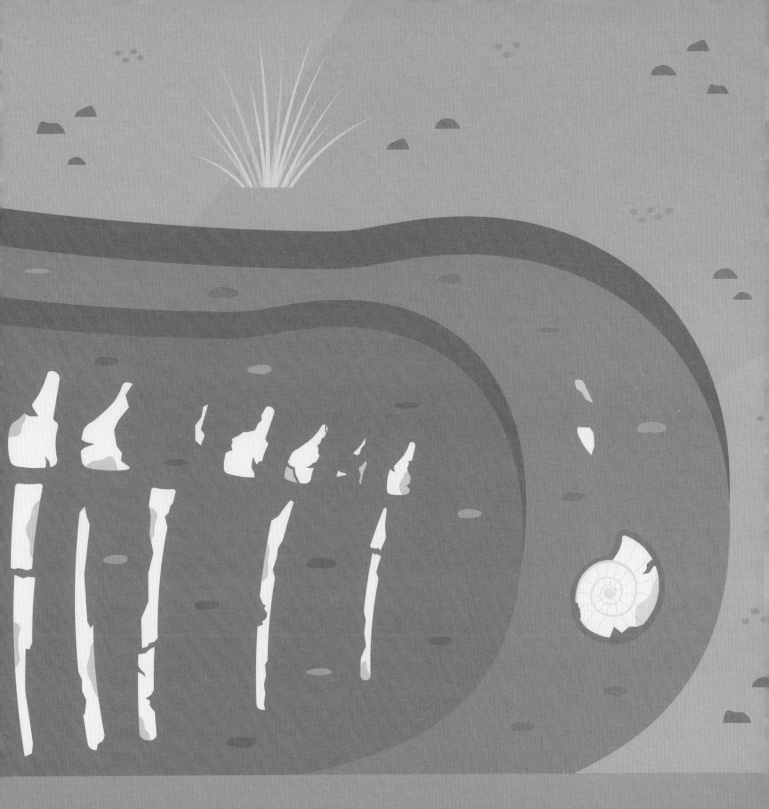

Ancient remains

Charles began to unearth bones – and lots of them. Soon he understood that his digs were uncovering the skeletons of large animals. The scientist found fossils belonging to mammals that had long since become extinct. It was like a giant jigsaw! Charles carefully collected and recorded each bone fragment so it could be sent back to England.

Chipping away

The fossilised bones were thousands of years old. One day on the coast of Argentina, Charles dug up a massive skull. It took him three hours to chip the skull out of the soft rock encasing it, and even longer to haul it back to the ship. The skull belonged to a giant ground sloth called *Megatherium*.

Mega-mammal

Until Charles' voyage, the giant ground sloth was unknown to science. When he studied the mammal's bones, Charles saw that it belonged to the same family as modern sloths. This creature however, was super-sized! When it was living over 10,000 years ago, an adult *Megatherium* would have been as big as today's car. Weighing in at a hefty six tonnes, it was the heaviest land mammal to ever have lived in South America.

Getting ideas

During the course of his digs, Charles would collect materials belonging to four different types of sloth species. He was incredibly excited by these discoveries. Finding out about animal families and studying extinct creatures such as the sloth helped the naturalist to form his very first theories about evolution.

The mystery of the friendly wolf

When the HMS *Beagle* sailed around the Falkland Islands, Charles was in for another surprise. A large, fox-like dog roamed the islands, the only native land mammal to be found in those parts. The creature was almost tame, daring to sniff around human camps without any signs of fear. Charles was puzzled by the friendly wolf – it didn't look like any other dog species he had seen on the mainland. He wondered how it could have got to the distant Falkland Islands. And why had no other mammals come with it? Although Charles pondered this question in his notebook, the mystery would not be solved until much later. Today DNA data has revealed that the mammal must have travelled to the islands on drifting icebergs or floating wood.

Thoughts and theories

Charles' travels were already setting his mind racing in all sorts of fascinating directions. The amazing wildlife he observed, the curious fossils he pulled out of the earth and the new specimens he collected posed all sorts of big questions. How did some animals adapt so cleverly to suit their environment? Why did some species thrive and others die out? Charles' trip would change the way he viewed the world forever.

Steamer ducks

While he was on the Falkland Islands, a funny little duck caught Charles' eye. The grey steamer duck was a paddling bird with a beak that was strong enough to crush shellfish – its favourite food. The steamer duck's wings were small and weak, however, making flying impossible.

Paddle and splash

When a steamer duck wants to get somewhere quickly, it raises itself up in the water and then uses its strong leg muscles to race along, flapping its wings and splashing noisily as it goes. Charles had to agree that the bird was well named – it moved just like a paddle steamer!

Wings and wonderings

The Falkland Islands were quiet and remote, and the weather was blustery and cold. Charles did not let this delay his explorations – he had so much to do! The birds in particular were astonishing. Many of them were thriving in great numbers, and yet several species were flightless. Why did birds have wings if they were not designed to fly?

Pondering penguins

Charles knew there were four types of penguin on the Falklands, but the Magellanic seems to be the only breed he encountered first-hand. The small, stripy-headed bird did not live on ice and snow like most penguin species, although it was similar in lots of other ways. The Magellanic was a strong swimmer, using its wings to scull through the water.

Places to go

Charles was very amused by the noisy Magellanic penguin. One day, he placed himself in between a penguin and the sea. The bird refused to change its path, waddling directly into the naturalist. It bravely pushed out its chest, nudging Charles to one side until it got through. It was as if the penguin had been programmed to make its direct route to the ocean.

Free to be flightless

Wings, it seemed, weren't always used for flying. Perhaps, on the Falkland Islands, some birds didn't need to fly? Charles thought about the steamer duck. With no predators to catch it, he could see that the bird was perfectly adapted to its island home.

Charles the hero

The HMS *Beagle* sailed on. One day, Charles and his shipmates had stopped to explore a tiny island when a huge chunk of ice broke off the face of a glacier nearby, crashing down into the ocean. The mass of ice was so vast it sent a huge wave rolling across the water, straight towards the *Beagle*'s rowing boats.

Charles to the rescue

The crew were in grave danger – without boats they would never be able to get back to their ship! The frozen waters were far too cold for a person to swim in. Charles rushed to the shore with two or three others and saved the boats from being washed away in the nick of time.

Darwin Sound

Captain FitzRoy was very grateful to Charles. Without the naturalist's quick thinking all of the men would surely have been marooned. In honour of his rescue, FitzRoy declared that the area should be known as Darwin Sound. The expanse of seawater near the southernmost tip of South America still bears this name today.

Magic in miniature

The mountains and forests of Brazil teem with life. Gigantic insects march across the forest floor, vivid tropical flowers fill the air with perfume and spectacular birds hop from branch to branch. Charles was captivated. One entry in his diary says he felt like a 'schoolboy in his holidays'. Perhaps it was because he had just encountered the most enchanting creature of all – a tiny, shimmering hummingbird.

A flash of colour

Many hummingbirds are small enough to fit in the palm of your hand, but they are stunning to observe. Dazzling, rainbow-like feathers sparkle in the sunlight as the bird uses its long beak to feed on nectar from plants and flowers.

Hover and flit

To a naturalist from England, the hummingbird must have been an astonishing sight. The little bird is able to hover in mid-air, like a puppet on an invisible string. Its wings move so incredibly fast they are scarcely visible to the naked eye, making a strange buzzing sound as the hummingbird flits from bloom to bloom.

Swallow-tailed hummingbird

Charles counted four different types of hummingbird as he climbed the Pedra da Gávea mountain. As he observed the birds he would have noticed that one species had an unusual tail. The swallow-tailed hummingbird has a deeply forked tail that is half as long as its body. This arrangement of feathers is perfectly suited to balancing the bird as it hovers in the air.

South America to the Galapagos Islands

Galapagos
Islands

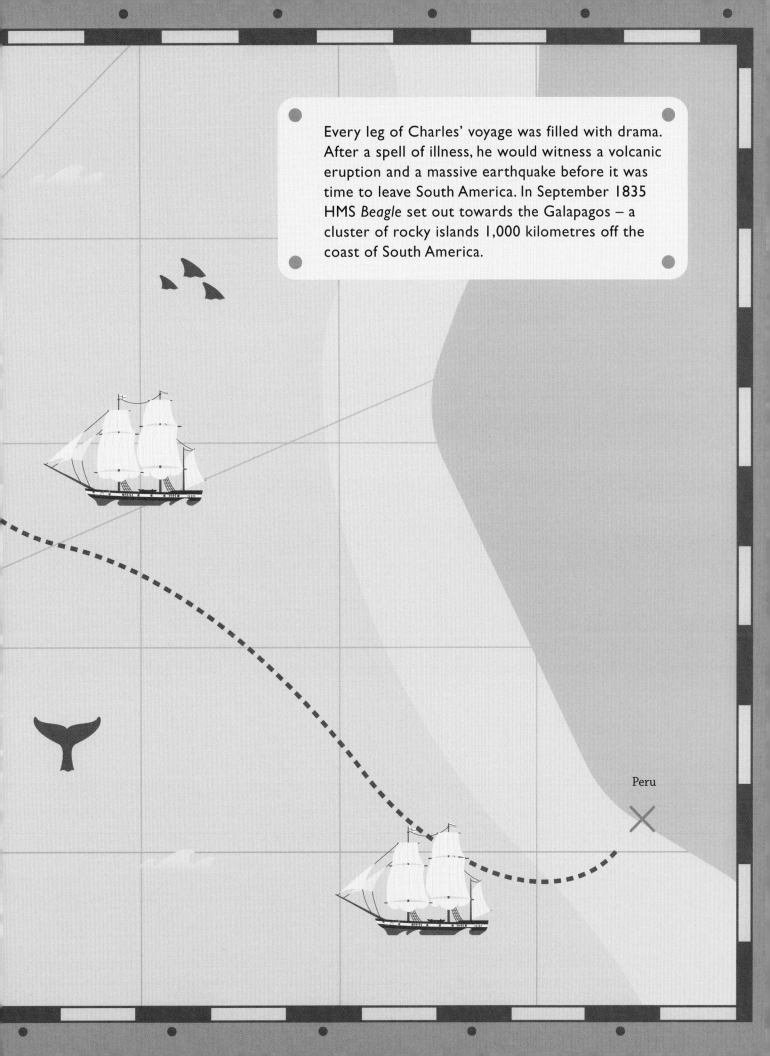

Every leg of Charles' voyage was filled with drama. After a spell of illness, he would witness a volcanic eruption and a massive earthquake before it was time to leave South America. In September 1835 HMS *Beagle* set out towards the Galapagos – a cluster of rocky islands 1,000 kilometres off the coast of South America.

Peru

Strange new world

The Galapagos must have seemed very barren and uninviting when HMS *Beagle* first arrived. The 18 larger islands in the group are covered with mounds of black lava rock, created by volcanic activity millions of years ago. The islands here are mostly within sight of each other and appear to have a similar climate.

Oasis in the ocean

The Galapagos Islands could not have been more remarkable! When Charles got ashore, he was in for a surprise. Rather than being barren and empty, the islands were rich with a staggering array of wildlife.

Living science

By now, Charles had been away from home for over three and a half years, but his enthusiasm for exploration was just as great as ever. He helped the *Beagle* crew to survey many of the islands, collecting specimens of rocks, plants and animals along the way. The notes that he made at this time were set to change the course of science forever.

Nothing to fear

Birds on the Galapagos were unused to seeing humans. When Charles approached, the creatures remained on their perches as if tame, unafraid of being studied in close quarters. The birds appeared to be broadly related to the species he had seen during his time in South America, but each had its unique qualities, too.

Birds of the Galapagos

Charles soon realised that several bird species had adapted their own special ways to stay safe and find food. Each type was perfectly suited to survival on its own local island.

Blue-footed booby

It would have been hard for Charles to miss the booby — a comical-looking seabird with bright blue feet. Although the booby is ungainly and clumsy on the land, when it dives into the ocean everything changes. The bird's feet act like flippers, pushing it through the water with ease.

Mockingbird

After a while, Charles noticed that the mockingbirds on several islands were slightly different from one another, despite living not far apart. The little birds had different beak lengths, and varied markings on their throats, breasts and wings.

Yellow warbler

The brightly-coloured yellow warbler is found all over the Americas, from Alaska in the north all the way down to Peru. Although warblers live across the Galapagos too, each bird population is slightly different on each of the different islands.

Grow your own way

In the Galapagos, all around Charles single species appeared to have developed and changed into lots of similar, but slightly different new ones. And it wasn't just birds – plants too were appearing in many forms across the three Galapagos zones:

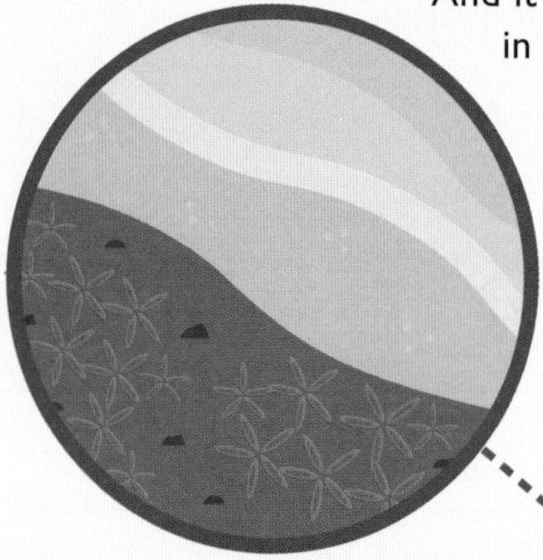

Coastal zone

A narrow area around the beaches of the islands. The plants that grow here are able to tolerate windy, salty conditions.

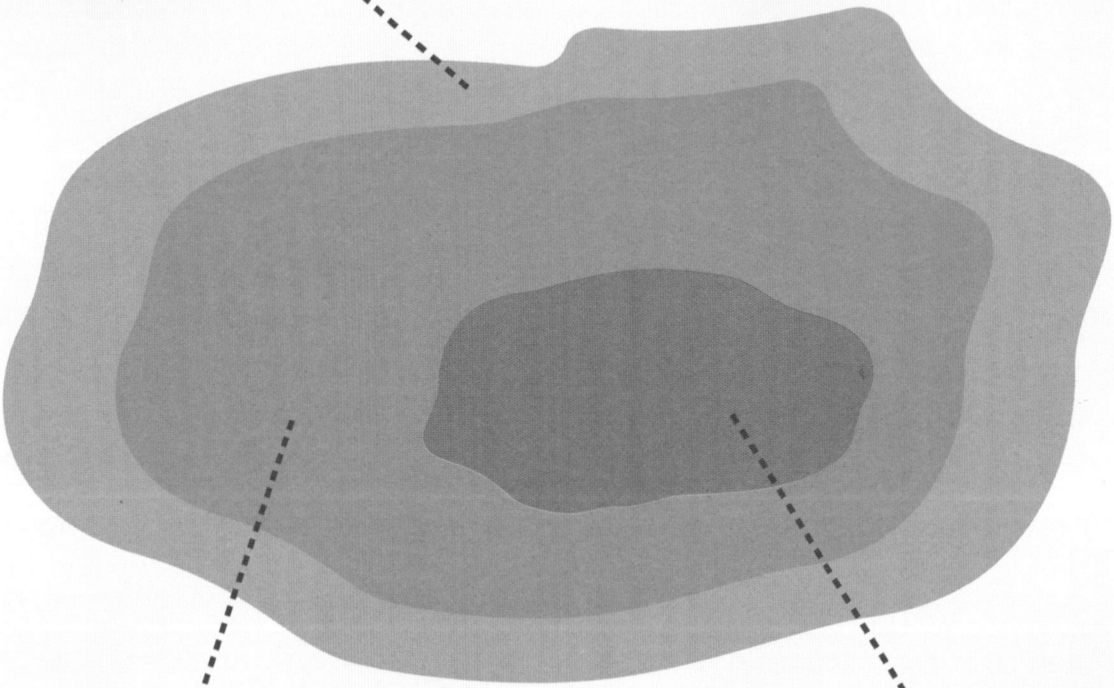

Arid zone

The largest area in the Galapagos is dry and desert-like. Spiky cacti and leafless shrubs are the only plants able to thrive here.

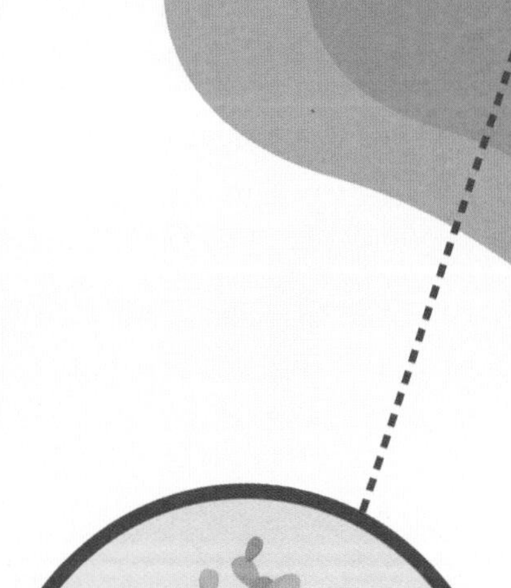

Humid zone

Only the biggest Galapagos islands have a humid zone. These higher areas are filled with dense forests of green *Scalesia* trees.

Spot the difference

Across the islands, plants vary in all sorts of ways – some are lofty and tall, others only grow as high as a small shrub. Even the shape and hairiness of the *Scalesia*'s leaf changes from forest to forest. Each type of plant is suited to the unique conditions in its own small corner of the Galapagos.

Adaptive radiation

The Galapagos Islands were formed when volcanoes erupted deep under the sea, creating a brand new place for life to grow. The islands are a long way from the mainland so cacti, moss and anything else that lives here is isolated from the rest of its species. Nowadays we know that these differences are examples of adaptive radiation – what happens when a plant or animal makes special adaptations to suit the climate and habitat that it lives in.

Bird watch

While he was roaming through the lush forests of the Galapagos, Charles turned his attention to the finches that used to flock and flutter everywhere that he went. During his stay on dry land the naturalist counted at least 13 different types of finch, each one slightly different to the rest. The specimens that he sent back to London would later help Charles unlock the mystery of evolution.

Truly unique

The types of finches that live in the Galapagos cannot be found anywhere else in the world. When the islands were first formed, a few birds must have found their way over to this new habitat from South America, perhaps blown across the ocean by storm winds.

Feeling peckish

The Galapagos are rich in plant and animal life, so there is lots of food available. Without any competition or many predators to watch out for, the finches have been able to survive and thrive. Over a long period of time, different bird colonies were able to adapt to suit the diet that was most plentiful in their area.

Spot the birdie

Charles was a constant collector. He carefully captured as many finches as he could, packing the specimens up so they could be sent back to London. He tagged each of the birds with a label, but he didn't think to write down which island he had found it on.

Close cousins

Charles' finches would go on to become world famous. The birds are often described as the inspiration behind his theory of evolution, but he didn't realise their importance until much later. When he got back to England, it was actually a bird expert called John Gould who explained to Charles that the finches were closely related.

Darwin's Finches

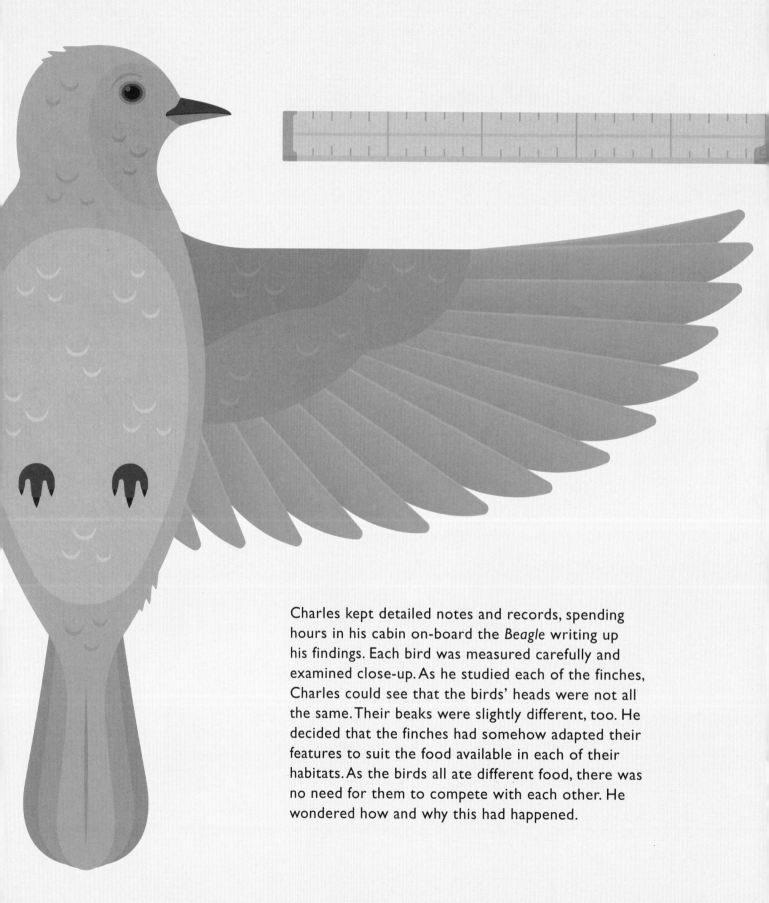

Charles kept detailed notes and records, spending hours in his cabin on-board the *Beagle* writing up his findings. Each bird was measured carefully and examined close-up. As he studied each of the finches, Charles could see that the birds' heads were not all the same. Their beaks were slightly different, too. He decided that the finches had somehow adapted their features to suit the food available in each of their habitats. As the birds all ate different food, there was no need for them to compete with each other. He wondered how and why this had happened.

Variations abound

It was surprising how many different types of finch could all come from the same South American ancestor. Some of the finches had developed large beaks that came to a sharp point. This helped them to crack open hard seeds. Others preferred to feed on finer seeds – their beaks were smaller to match (see overleaf).

As well as head and beak variations, there were other differences, too. Some had larger bodies and longer tails, some grew feathers in muted colours while others even warbled their own unique song.

The finches would later help Charles to come up with a new idea called natural selection. Over time, the plants and animals that adapt quickly to match changes in their environment are the species that tend to survive. Darwin's finches did just this when they first arrived in the Galapagos. If they hadn't adapted their beaks and feeding habits, they might have died out.

Beak up!

Seed eaters

There are over a dozen closely related finch species on the Galapagos. Most of the ground-dwelling birds feed on nuts and seeds. Their beaks are shaped to suit the size and hardness of the seeds available in the area around them. The islands of the Galapagos are too far apart for the finches to fly between and breed with each other.

Cactus and fruit eaters

The cactus ground finch has a very particular diet. It uses its beak to feed on spiky plants such as the prickly pear cactus. The smart bird has learned to get all sorts of nourishment from the plant – pecking at its pulp, fruits and insects feeding on the cactus flowers. Other finches have adapted to survive on softer foods such as berries.

Insect eaters

Many tree finches are better adapted to nibble on creepy crawlies rather than seeds. They have special grasping or probing beaks that can easily pluck an insect out of a tight space and then swallow it down. The woodpecker finch has refined its skills to such a degree, it is even able to use tools. The bird has learned how to snap a twig down to the right length and then use it as a spear to harpoon a bug for supper. Impressive!

Land of the giants

Charles described the Galapagos as a 'little world within itself'. Huge reptiles also roamed on the isles – giant tortoises with wrinkled faces and enormous, hard shells. Charles timed their walking speed, watched them lay eggs and measured how much water they drank.

Dome-shaped tortoise

It didn't take long for Charles to work out that there were two main types of tortoise on the islands. One type had a dome-shaped shell with a short neck and legs. The front of this tortoise's shell was closed, allowing it to shrink up inside its harder outer casing if it needed to protect itself. The dome-shaped tortoise was the closest to the tortoises on the mainland.

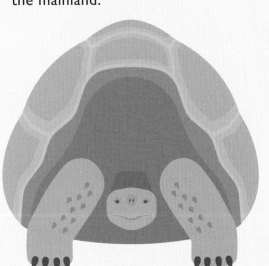

Saddle-back tortoise

The other tortoise that Charles observed had a shell that rose up at the front like a saddle. This type was more aggressive, stretching out its long neck and legs when it wanted to gain extra height. It was mostly found in drier areas on the Galapagos islands. Despite its longer neck and legs, the saddle-back was the smaller of the two tortoise types.

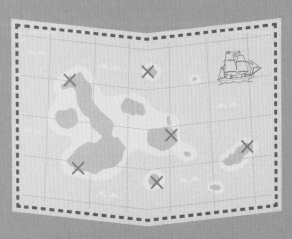

On the map

Charles wasn't the only one to notice the different shell shapes across the islands – the local people were aware of it, too. They told the naturalist that the reptiles developed slightly differently on each of the Galapagos islands. Some even claimed that they could pinpoint where a tortoise lived just by looking at its shell!

Location, location

Dome-shaped tortoises do not have to forage hard for their food. They live on islands where there is lots of dense undergrowth near the ground. All the tortoise has to do is crawl along with its head low, munching on anything it passes. Saddle-back tortoises are adapted to live on lower ground where there is less lush vegetation. The rise in its shell gives it the space to lift its head up and eat from bushes, shrubs and cacti.

Mega monsters

Land iguana

There are two main types of iguana on the Galapagos. The land iguana lives inland, feeding on plants and leaves. The lumbering yellow lizard spends its mornings basking in the sun. When night falls it scuttles into its underground burrow. This helps the iguana to retain its body temperature and store the energy it needs to move.

Charles was fascinated by life in all of its forms, but the iguanas of the Galapagos Islands put his love of nature to the test. The scaly reptiles patrolled nearly every beach, tongues flicking and tails sweeping left and right. At first, Charles was horrified.

Marine iguana

The marine iguana is the only sea-going lizard in the world. Charles was not taken with its inky scales and creepy, wide-set eyes. He described it as a 'disgusting' and 'clumsy' creature. When a marine iguana takes to the ocean however, Charles could not have been more wrong. The lizard has adapted its body to swim through water with grace and ease, using its sharp teeth to nibble algae and seaweed from the rocks as it passes by.

Food for thought

In October 1835 it was time for HMS *Beagle* to leave the Galapagos Islands and continue its great voyage. Charles' visit had only lasted a few short weeks, but he had made all sorts of fascinating discoveries. He and his servant, Syms Covington, had collected many samples to share with other scientists back home. During his time on the ship he logged and packed up a dove, four snakes, two owls, a buzzard and many other creatures. There were fewer insects to preserve however, a feature he noted across the Galapagos. Charles had also tried to bring back a sample of every plant he saw in flower.

Time for change

As the ship sailed on, Charles had more time to study the birds, reptiles and plant specimens that had been collected. It was only then that he began to properly notice how many species were unique to the islands. Did Charles wish he could go back for a second look? Perhaps. Later he would write, 'it is the fate of every voyager when he has just discovered what object in any place is more particularly worth of his attention, to be hurried from it.'

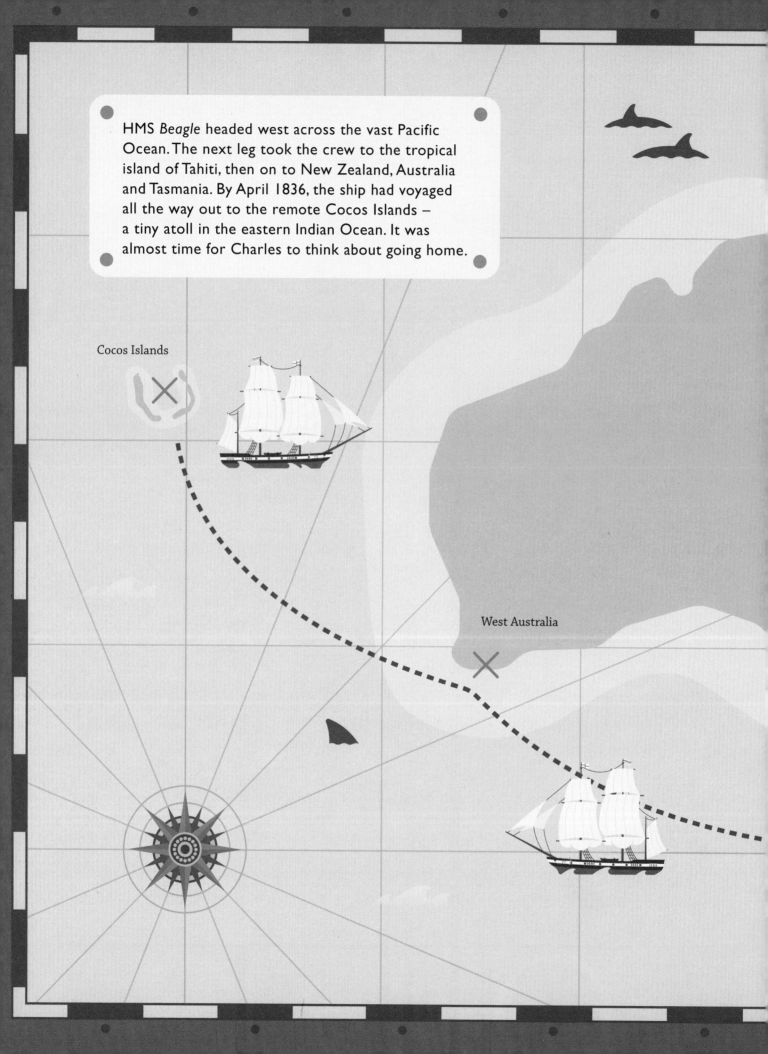

HMS *Beagle* headed west across the vast Pacific Ocean. The next leg took the crew to the tropical island of Tahiti, then on to New Zealand, Australia and Tasmania. By April 1836, the ship had voyaged all the way out to the remote Cocos Islands — a tiny atoll in the eastern Indian Ocean. It was almost time for Charles to think about going home.

Cocos Islands

West Australia

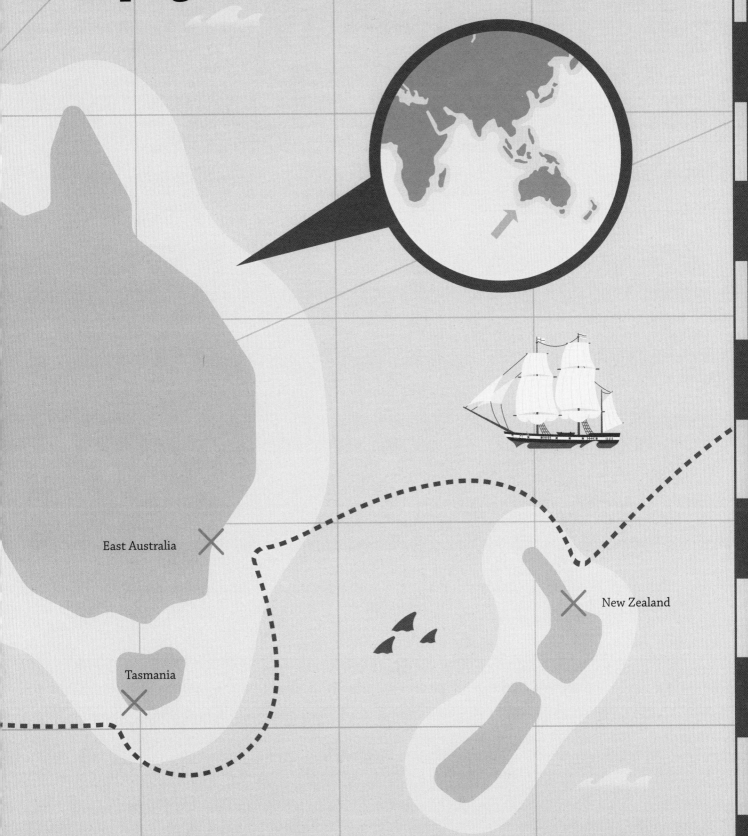

Galapagos to the Cocos Islands

Fantastical creatures

During his visit to Australia, Charles was keen to get a feel for the country. This vast, foreign land was home to all sorts of fantastical creatures. The kangaroo, wallaby, koala and many other species could not be found anywhere else on the planet. Imagine what Charles must have thought when he stumbled across a duck-billed platypus for the very first time! The strange little mammal has the flat beak of a duck, the furry body of an otter and the wide tail of a beaver. Charles noted that the platypus lived in one small corner of the world, expertly suited to a life spent diving in the creeks and streams of the southern hemisphere.

Reef revelations

After the vast spaces of Australia and New Zealand, Captain FitzRoy set a course for a tiny lagoon – a circle of reef known as the Cocos Islands. The reef was lined with sandy beaches and coconut trees, but just below the waves a whole new kingdom awaited. Charles waded into the water and gazed at the spectacular coral formation below. Fish darted in and out of seaweed fronds, sea cucumbers sat plump and frilly, and starfish stretched lazily across the rocks.

Birth of an atoll

The reef was home to a host of astonishing marine life. Bright parrotfish flashed in the sunlight as the coral swayed back and forth. Charles began to wonder how such an amazing ecosystem had been created. He started to form a theory that the reef had originally grown up around an extinct volcano. When the volcano sank into the ocean, only the isolated circle remained.

Beware of the crab

The Cocos Islands were certainly beautiful, but life on such a remote reef was not without its drawbacks. Aside from fish, food was very scarce – the locals' only native land vegetable was the coconut. Charles was startled to see that many of the palm trees were guarded by immense crabs that grew to 'a monstrous size'.

Coconut crabs

Charles had encountered the world's largest land invertebrate – the 1-metre-long coconut crab, a rare creature that lives on coral atolls and tropical islands. He observed how the crab could climb high up into the trees, breaking open coconut shells with its mighty pincers. At that time very little scientific information would have been known about this formidable species.

Pincer power

Charles would have been wise to observe the coconut crab from a safe distance. As well as being super-sized, its massive pincers are strong enough to crush six times its own bodyweight! The naturalist thought that the species only lived in a very small area in the Pacific, but now we know that it can be found more widely.

No limits

Coconut crabs are a type of hermit crab. When it is small, it has to find a shell to move into. It will stay there feeding and growing, until the shell becomes too tight to live in. After about a year, the coconut crab throws off its portable home and allows its body to harden. Without a house to fit into, it is now free to grow as big as it likes.

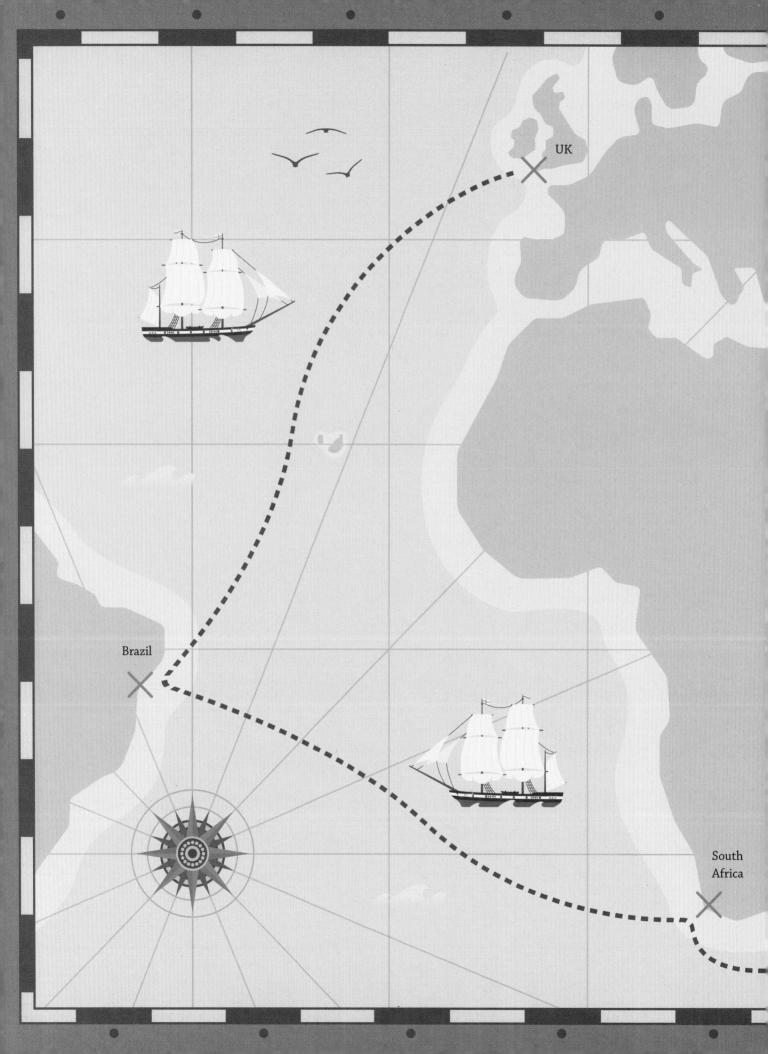

Cocos to England

The HMS *Beagle's* epic journey was nearly at an end. The ship continued west towards Cape Town, perched on the southern tip of Africa. By now Darwin was ready to get home, but first the crew needed to make one last stop in Brazil so that Captain FitzRoy could take some more surveys. In August 1836 it was finally time to set sail directly for England. Charles was delighted.

Cocos Islands

Starry night

As he made his way home, Charles spent many nights at sea reflecting on his adventures. After nearly five years of collecting he needed to plan how he was going to sort and organise his hundreds of specimens. It would soon be time to start putting his discoveries together into a pattern – all sorts of ideas must have been whirling around in Charles' mind. As he sailed through the southern hemisphere one last time, the naturalist enjoyed standing on deck and thinking, gazing up at the starry sky.

Show me the way

Stars have been important to sailors since ancient times. For thousands of years, they have relied on the night sky to help them navigate through leagues of endless ocean. Bright pole stars were used as locators because they didn't disappear below the horizon.

Southern stars

As the Earth rotates, the part of the sky that we can see changes, but this does not mean that stargazers in the southern and northern hemispheres eventually get to see the same constellations. While some stars can be seen both north and south of the Equator, others can only be viewed in each hemisphere.

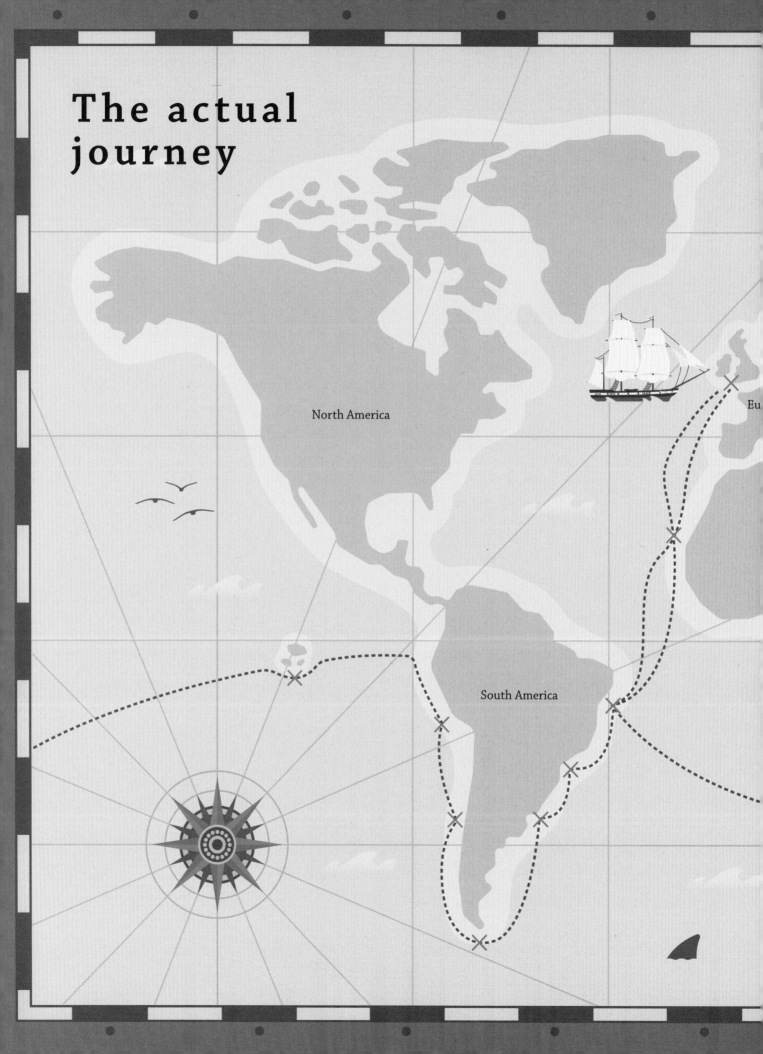

The actual journey

North America

South America

Eu

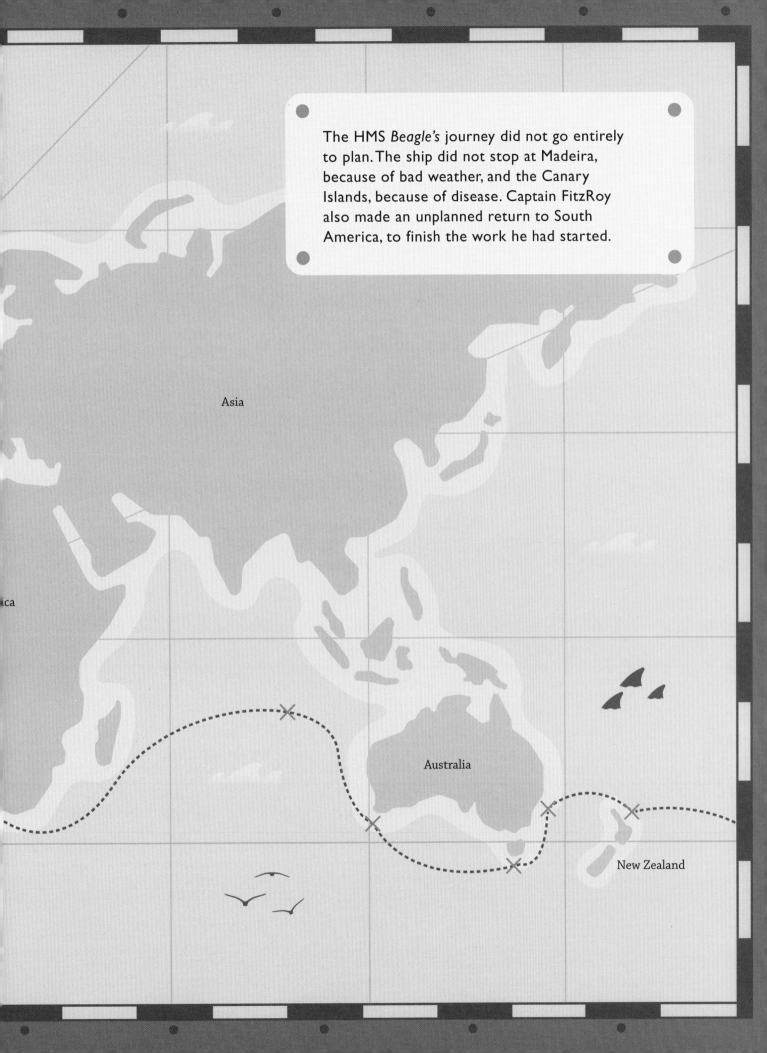

The HMS *Beagle's* journey did not go entirely to plan. The ship did not stop at Madeira, because of bad weather, and the Canary Islands, because of disease. Captain FitzRoy also made an unplanned return to South America, to finish the work he had started.

Asia

Australia

New Zealand

The last leg

Charles had been away from his friends and his family for a very long time, but he had always made the effort to send long letters back to England. He wrote to his siblings, father, and scientific colleagues. Now he could finally contemplate being with them in person! He must have wondered what it would be like to see their faces again.

Pit stop

The return trip to England would not be swift. HMS *Beagle* spent several, long months edging its way back up towards the Equator. From time to time, Charles and the crew had the opportunity to make a brief stopover. During the journey back, they visited Mauritius, St Helena Island and the Azores.

Now or never

On the way back past South America, Captain FitzRoy felt concerned that he might have made some mistakes when he was charting maps of San Salvador. He made a decision to go back and do some corrections. While the crew set to work on this, Charles had one last chance to explore the forests of Brazil.

Feeling green

Charles was relieved when Captain FitzRoy finally decided that he was ready to leave Brazil, even though he knew that the journey would not be enjoyable. Despite his years living on the ocean waves, the naturalist still suffered from terrible seasickness. He couldn't wait to put an end to the 'tedious misery of loss of time, health and comfort'.

Home sweet home

After a voyage of four years, nine months and five days, HMS *Beagle* sailed into British waters. Charles would have been thrilled to enjoy the familiar sights and smells of home. He had left England as a naive young man – now he was returning as a mature naturalist eager to test out his ground-breaking new ideas.

Homecoming

FitzRoy, Charles and all the crew had one last challenge to face – a rainstorm which drenched HMS *Beagle* on its way back into port. The ship finally arrived at Falmouth Docks at nine o'clock on a dark, dreary evening. Charles did not waste any time. He said a brief farewell to his shipmates, then set off for his family home.

Surprise!

It took Charles a little while to travel all the way up to Shrewsbury. When he finally arrived home in the dead of night, his family were fast asleep in bed! Charles waited until the next morning before casually strolling into the dining room while his father and sisters were eating their breakfast. Everyone leapt out of their chairs, shrieking with delight to see Charles back home at last.

Back to work

The HMS *Beagle* served Captain FitzRoy well, but the journey had taken its toll on the vessel. The ship needed urgent repairs. In November 1836, the *Beagle* was given a refit. By July 1837, she was ready to set sail once more. A new captain, John Wickham, was put in charge of her third and final voyage.

A life's work

Charles never forgot his journey on HMS *Beagle*. Back home in England, he started the slow process of shaping his experiences into a series of scientific breakthroughs that would change modern thinking forever. Many years later, when Charles was an elderly man, he wrote down what the expedition had meant to him:

'The voyage of the *Beagle* has been by far the most important event in my life, and has determined my whole career. Everything about which I thought or read was made to bear directly on what I had seen or was likely to see; and this habit of mind was continued during the five years of the voyage. I feel sure that it was this training which has enabled me to do whatever I have done in science.'

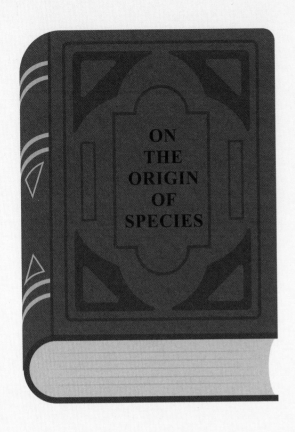

On the Origin of Species

When Charles got home, he spent many years examining his collections and showing them to other experts in geology and natural history. He soon became a respected scientist in his own right. It would be twenty years, in 1859, however, before Charles felt ready to publish his theory about natural selection. It would be called *On the Origin of Species*.

'The most dangerous man in England'

With natural selection, only the species best suited to their environment will survive. This was an outrageous revelation for Victorian society because it challenged the common belief that God made the Earth and its animals. Theologians referred to Darwin as the 'most dangerous man in England.' Nevertheless, in 1871, Charles went one step further – he proposed that humans and apes were both descended from the same common ancestor.

Game changer

Charles' voyage on the *Beagle* exposed him to nature in all of its extraordinary variety. This rich harvest was the proof he needed to show how natural selection worked. It explained the difference between the Galapagos finches and offered up all sorts of other ways that species adapt to suit their environment. Natural selection supported Charles' theory of evolution.

Darwin's legacy

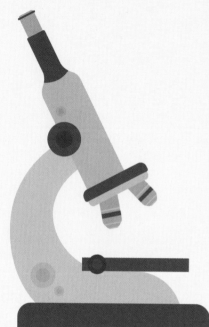

At first Charles' research was very unpopular, but it got people talking and thinking. Over time, the scientific world would be ready to use modern technology to prove his theory of evolution by natural selection. Scientists had the tools they needed to group animals and plants in families, then study the features that had enabled them to survive.

It's in the genes

Investigation into how features are passed on in nature developed into the science of genetics. Scientists have now learned that every form of life carries a chemical code inside its cells. This is called DNA. It is passed on from generation to generation. By studying the genetic codes of Darwin's finches we can now prove Charles' notion that the birds did indeed descend from the same ancestor.

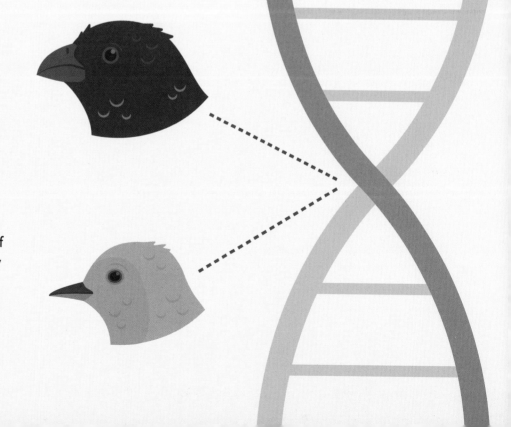

Descent of man

Charles was a shy, nervous person, and so he didn't like to argue about his theories in public. Although many fiercely objected to the idea that humans evolved from apes, his thinking is now widely accepted. Tests show that our genetic code is only one or two per cent different from chimpanzees – our closest cousins.

Journey of discovery

Although some still disagree with Charles' big ideas, no one can deny how important and influential his work has been. He created a revolution in how human beings see and think about the world. Charles encouraged science to leap forward in every direction – testing his findings and moving them on. He was the greatest naturalist of his time… and perhaps all time.

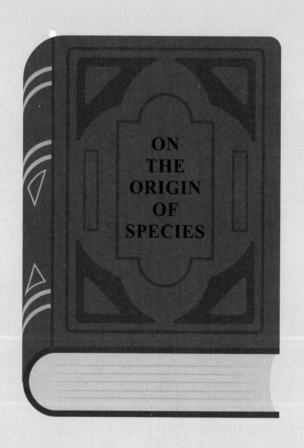